THE POWER THAT CONTROLS WEALTH

Discover what makes for creation and perpetuation of wealth

George Donald

Copyright
© George Donald 2022

All rights reserved

Acknowledgement

I begin by thanking God almighty for keeping my pen flowing till the end of this work. I thank Him for all His provision and guidance, may His name be praised.

My thanks also goes to my lovely wife, Jennifer Donald. She's indeed the best gift I have ever had. She has been of immense support to all areas of my life and I'm very grateful for that.

This book wouldn't have seen the light of the day if not for the overwhelming support from Mr John Patterson, my mentor and friend; Mr Edwin Thomas; Sir William Thomas and Steve Jones. I can't imagine how life would be without you guys.

I wouldn't make the mistake of not recognizing my students from all parts of the world. Thanks for your continuous support and most especially, for your feedback and reviews. To be sincere, there wouldn't be George Donald in the writing world without you guys. Thank you so much.

Time wouldn't permit me to start thanking people one after the other, so I'm saying a big thanks to all who have been of help in one way or the other. I sincerely appreciate it.

Dedication

This book is specially dedicated everyone aspiring to gain financial liberty

Table of contents

INTRODUCTION

Chapter one : Creating A Wealth Supporting Mindset

- Money First
- The more you work, the more money you make
- Money is an object for gratification of taste
- Wealth is by luck
- the more wealth you accumulate, the more your level of insecurity
- The wealthier one becomes, the harder it becomes for him to serve God
- Wealth is for some special people

Chapter two: Understanding The Nature of Wealth

- What does it mean to be wealthy
- Exploring the various pools of intangible wealth
- Knowledge/ wisdom
- Influence
- Inspiration
- Trust

Chapter three: Planning your wealth

- Thirteenth things you must do to be rich

Chapter Four: Steps to Wealth Creation

- Discover a problem
- Design a solution
- Sell your solution
- 6 Secrets of massive sales

PART B: WEALTH PERPETUATION

Chapter five: Adopting a Healthy Finance Management

- Earning
- Spending
- Saving
- Investment of savings

Chapter six : Keep It Steady

Chapter seven: Secure Your Wealth

THE RIGHT PLACE TO START

INTRODUCTION

Due to the very numerous importance of money and how ambiguous the subject of wealth creation seems to be, there is every need to guide the society towards the mastery of the subject. Indeed, there are so many misconceptions revolving around the system and until these misconceptions are cleared, it will continue to be a serious problem. Humanity needs to be clearly taught that wealth creation is not a rocket science, that all it requires is just the right knowledge coupled with its right application for the right purpose and at the right time.

You must have admired riches at one point or the other, thus the buying of this book and am assuring you that you have made the right choice. This book is a product of many years of experience and each chapter is carefully written to serve as a step closer to your desired state of financial freedom.

The book begins with a mind preparatory chapter for the creation of the needed mindset for wealth creation. Then, to throwing light on the various forms of wealth that must be acquired first before the acquisition of financial wealth. Going further, I also shared with you the right ways of increasing your earning as well as some effective finance management processes.

Understanding that to make wealth is not more important than remaining wealthy, I further shared some of the things you need to do in order to remain financially free even when you no longer have to work.

I advise you that you study this book with all your attention and do so with a pen and paper so you can jot down some important points.

Happy reading!

Chapter one

Creating A Wealth Supporting Mindset

Before a farmer plants any seed, the first inclination he would have is to clear all the existing vegetation capable of undermining the yield of his new crop. Doing this gives him the first required space before other planting operations can commence.

An adult's mind is the same as that piece of land that requires thorough clearing before any new seed can survive. The only difference is that in human mind, what is always done is selective clearing where you leave what is needed and remove that which is not.

All that is in your mind, whether conscious or subconscious, is what designs your belief system, your belief system designs your thought pattern, your thought pattern designs your attitude, and finally, your attitude designs your results in life. From this, it can be seen that it all begins in the mind. You're a product of your mindset. Being rich or poor is a result of your kind of mindset. Your mind is that powerful! It is in the spirit of this understanding that I decided not only to include this chapter in this book but to make it the first. All the life-changing lessons engraved in this book will remain barren of results like a land starved of water if this chapter fails to fulfill its purpose, which is removing all the elements of your mind that have been antagonizing your efforts to create wealth. Having said that, I am sure I have captured your full attention.

One thing you believe or do not believe about wealth is capable of keeping you away from it for a lifetime. The Belief system, on the other hand, is usually a function of the things we know as well as the things we do not know. This means that we agree or disagree with something, not only because of what we know about that, but also as a result of what we do not know. To make it simpler, our agreeing or disagreeing with something is either based on what we know about that thing or what we do not know. In other to set the balance we need for this journey to the endless stream of wealth, I would need you to pause for a while and do this task:

Write down all the lessons you have learnt so far about money, the things you like about money and the things you don't like; the things you often hear about money and from there, separate the ones you believe to be true from the ones you don't believe. Gathering all this information, try drawing a general conclusion.

Well done, if you have done this task. Next, in two minutes or more, think about your financial life. Has it gotten to your desired level? Maybe, No. But, whichever way, if I am to go through what you have written in the little task above, I can show you where the problem is. I will be presenting to you deep secrets capable of taking you to that desired level, however, some of the things I will be sharing might not sound too good to you, which you always have the right to discard.

So we begin. Here is a list of some of the ideologies that regulate the way people relate with money and subsequently, whether they will be able to accumulate wealth .

1. MONEY FIRST

My grandfather once told me a story of a certain rich man who was so generous and there are five beggars that come to his house to beg everyday for their daily bread. For each day, the rich man would either give them food or some piece of silver, or both.

One day, the rich man called the five beggars and said to them, "I will soon leave this world for the world of the dead and I have a gift for each of you, so, come with me to my treasure room. The treasure room was a demarcation from his bedroom and was built in such a way that no one can notice it except the old man.

Taking them to the treasure room, he said to them, "Look, there are bags of gold and by my right are scrolls. In each scroll is written the seven laws of gold. Go now and choose for yourself what is more important to you, either a bag of gold, or a scroll of the seven laws of gold."

Without hesitation, the beggars all rushed to get bags of gold except one who happens to be the youngest among them, who went for the scroll instead of the bag of gold.

The rich old man, surprised but impressed by the boy's decision, called out to him while he was leaving alongside others and said, "Come and tell me why you would rather choose the scroll instead of a bag of gold."

Then he answered, "I thought to myself that if I should study and master the seven laws of gold, which I believe was what made you the richest man my eyes have ever seen, I will be able to earn my own gold, not just in bag but in bags."

Again, the old man asked, "Did you not consider how difficult it will be for you to cope until you are able to earn your own gold since I will be leaving you soon for the world of the dead?"

Then he replied, "I thought of that but I decided that I will begin to study what is in the scroll and also implement them as soon as I learn them."

The old man became more surprised at the poor boy's level of wisdom. Then he asked further, "How about your father?" To which he answered that he is dead. He also asked about his mother and he told him she's dead too. He told him he is an only child and did not know any of his parents. That it was his aunty who raised him and they have been living together until war broke out in their kingdom. Being much tender that time, he was displaced and could not find his way back.

"Quite pathetic," the old man said pitifully. "How did you get to this kingdom?"

"As I was crying because everyone had left me, a warrior came by and picked me up. I guess he was too compassionate to hurt such a cute innocent boy, so he took me home. According to him, he did that because he thought that my parents must have been killed in the war. I began to live with his family and he was so kind to me, giving me all the care a father would give to his son.

Few years later, the king of that kingdom waged another war against their neighboring kingdom. Unfortunately, he was one of the victims of the war and that was how the king's greed robbed me of his care and love.

"After he was buried, his wife and children began treating me like a slave. They made my life so miserable that I had attempted suicide twice. As hope for a better future was still burning so hot in my heart, I decided to run away to a place where none of them could find me and that was how I came here."

When he finished narrating his story, silence filled the room for some seconds. Then the old man took a deep breath.

"So, you passed through all these, you're really destined for greatness. And by choosing this scroll of the seven laws of gold, you have proven to have chosen process over result and for that, I shall stake all I have to see your greatness come through. You shall live with me henceforth and we shall study the laws together until you master it all.

"I bless the gods of our land for they have given me a worthy hand to commit all I have labored for before joining my ancestors since I have no child of my own"

The boy was drenched in his tears as he knelt down and began thanking him. That was how they began to live together.

Few days later, after they finished eating dinner, the boy asked him why he did not tell the other beggars to choose the scroll instead of the bag of gold since it is better.

Then he replied, "It is not within the context of the law of the universe to influence any man's decision. If not, we wouldn't have been given the power of choice in the first place.

"If the foolish beggars had asked me, I would have chosen what is best for them just like the universe would do whenever we are in need of the right wisdom and call for assistance. My son, whenever you're being asked to choose one out of too many good things and you don't know which one is the best, it is always wise that you plead with the person to help you. In your humility, you might find favor in his eyes and he will help you to make the best decision."

Having said that, he paused for a while. Then he continued, facing him directly this time.

"The entire universe is built upon the law of process and that is why it is so pleased with those who are keen to master them more than they chase after results. Those who master these laws shall dine with rulers of the universe and only God can limit the level of power they can manifest. Every manifestation of this world is simply based on these laws.

"My late father was able to summarize the law as follows, "Every manifestation in this world is a function of an established condition" and since I learnt that, I became more concerned about those conditions.

"Nothing happens in this life except the condition for it is established. If you are poor, it is because of an already established condition, likewise if you are rich. If you are poor and you find a bag of gold just like your friends, that gold is a result of a condition that someone else has established and because you can not be able to maintain that condition, all the gold will leave you and you will go back begging again. I can assure you that this is what will happen to them.

"Whatever you admire in this life, wealth, health, happiness or power all have a condition and once the condition is established, the impartial universe will bring it to you. So just like you've chosen to learn what it takes to create wealth instead of having just a bite of someone else's wealth, do the same when you crave for power, true happiness."

It was one of the most educating stories I have ever heard and I still hold on to its numerous life-changing lessons up till today. Money, happiness, name it, does not come first, you get it after a condition has been established. For money, among the things you need before its acquisition is gathering the right knowledge just like you're doing now.

One thing you need to know is that you must be able to deliver to a reasonable extent in your area of specialization before you can earn from it. The market has no room for newbies; it's either you can give them what they want or you can't go home with what you want. It's as simple as that. People can be generous, and can willingly throw out money, but that's not when it comes to buying. Everybody wants to make the best out of his money and nobody is ready to pay for junk. You need to get the knowledge and then render the service before you get paid.

In addition, money is simply a reward for the service rendered and the amount of such reward you get is a function of how much the service is being rendered in terms of the number of people it serves; how well the

service is being rendered; the time in which it is rendered and the location. Have you now seen that money doesn't just come unless certain factors are being put in place. Do you still remember the "conditions" in the law of process as used in the above story, they're the same thing as these factors.
In summary, your main focus should be to do it better and once you achieve that, money will not be a problem.

2. THE MORE YOU WORK, THE MORE MONEY YOU MAKE.

People with this mindset are known for working and working and most times running into frustration especially when they measure their result against the energy they exert. They often don't know or don't believe in other ways of making money. The truth is that no one has ever made wealth through their work alone.

That is the first mindset you need to really work on _in case you already have it. Truely, the more you work, the more money you make, but not enough to accumulate into wealth. Your effort alone can not bring you Wealth. Wealth creation is impossible unless you employ some other agents and let me quickly tell you the most powerful and reliable of them. That is MONEY itself. Money is so powerful that it can replicate your effort in one hundred places. Imagine having a hundred workers working for you.

Instead of saving and saving yet remaining at that same level, why not put in more money to expand that business? Why rely on those old equipment when you can buy better ones that will make the work easier, faster and more efficient? Your profit might be way too small for the equipment, but you can save for it. Why do the whole job alone when you can employ more labor? Have you ever wondered why people work more and earn less as sole proprietors whereas in partnership, everybody is putting in moderate effort and yet, going home with more pay? The reason is simple and it all lies in their various levels of resources utilization. More resources are being employed in partnership business unlike sole proprietorship.

Apart from our limited individual ability, time is one of the most limiting factors in everything we do as humans. We only have twenty-four hours everyday and nothing more. Out of that twenty-four hours, we can only work for just a fraction of it, say ten to twelve hours under most unstandardized conditions. However, with money, one can work for a thousand hours in just eight hours by simply employing others to join him. Watch the magic, based on agreement, you're only going to give out a little fraction of what your workers generated as their salaries and the rest of the revenue becomes yours! That is how money has helped many firm owners to earn in one month what they can not earn in ten years should they work alone.

WEALTH CREATION IS IMPOSSIBLE UNLESS YOU EMPLOY SOME OTHER AGENTS AND AMONG THE MOST POWERFUL AND RELIABLE OF THEM IS MONEY

---

3. MONEY IS AN OBJECT FOR THE GRATIFICATION OF TASTE.

If your only motivation for earning is because of the gratifying effects of money, your chance of being really rich will be greatly maligned. Let's think of a certain man who likes maize so much. Then he cleared his piece of land, ran around and got some maize seeds and gladly planted his land with it. The seeds germinated and in a few months later, ready for harvest. Then the man said, "oh how sweet maize tastes" and began eating and eating until the whole garden was finished. Then he began to starve until the next season.

This is the same attitude of many people towards money_ earn, spend all, and then remain broke till they earn again. To make the matter worse, most people in this category are low income earners and they will never go beyond that level.

Money is not only an object for gratification, it is also an object for the accumulation of more money. Imbibe this ideology and you will see how your financial life will be transformed afterwards. To this, out of whatever you earn, (either big or small) save for yourself a fraction that will be reinvested for the expansion of your earning. The fastest and easiest way to accumulate more money is not by hoarding it but by investing it. However, you have to start from saving until you have enough for investment.

The most difficult challenge to saving is the numerous needs that awaits every penny that enters one's pocket, but the question you should always ask yourself is whether spending all will be enough to attend to all of them. The answer will always be hell no. So each time you earn some money, write down your needs in their order of importance, the most important being the first, followed by the next until the last and the least important need. Begin to attend to as much as you can starting from the most important and that should be done after you have saved the fraction you wish to save. It will be difficult when you are first forming the habit but trust me, you will soon master it and you will be glad you did. Time will even come when you will be saving at so much ease that you don't feel it anymore.

4. WEALTH IS BY LUCK

The world is full of people who are experts in justifying their inefficiency. A man picks up a dream, disciplines himself, sacrifices pleasure, invests everything, and labor everyday until he actualizes the dream. Then, lazy neighbors will begin to say he is lucky. Wealth is never by luck. You can be more privileged than others but that is not a guarantee for wealth. Think about the lottery winners. Research has shown that it is only very few out of hundreds of them that later became wealthy. Money can enter your hand by luck but it takes more than luck to sustain it.

To prove to you that money making is not by luck, think of any wealthy person you know. Make out time to study everything about him in the area of money and try to imitate him. If you follow it right, the result you will get in six months time will surprise you.

MONEY CAN ENTER YOUR HAND BY LUCK BUT IT TAKES MORE THAN LUCK TO SUSTAIN IT.

---

5. THE MORE WEALTH YOU ACCUMULATE, THE MORE YOUR LEVEL OF INSECURITY

There is always a price for everything, being poor and being rich alike. While a poor man is paying the price of an empty stomach, a rich man is paying to secure his abundance. While a poor man can walk hundred miles alone without fear of being robbed, a rich man can not, he will need security. While a rich man is afraid that he might lose his money due to the economic downturn, the poor man doesn't have anything to lose. All these and lots more on the side of a poor man could seem like a reward for being poor while those on the rich man's side is a price. Now, if you're being asked to choose, would you choose the poor man's reward over the rich's price? I don't know for you but I would rather pay more and more price on the side of the rich than to be a poor man.

The truth is that in a real sense, being a poor man comes with a greater price. Think about having to struggle life out of yourself before you could pay your basic bills. Imagine having to settle for the cheapest meal which you don't like just because you can't pay for a decent meal. What about not being able to get your desired clothes? None of these is a problem on the side of a rich man, his money has offered him security to all that. Therefore, money is a source of security and not the other way round.

MONEY IS A SOURCE OF SECURITY AND NOT THE OTHER WAY ROUND.

---

6. THE WEALTHIER ONE BECOMES, THE HARDER IT BECOMES FOR HIM TO SERVE GOD

Thinking about all the wonderful things that money can do in serving God and for humanity at large, I see it as a display of ignorance to see its acquisition as evil. The truth is that without money, serving God will be extremely difficult. The bible charges us to help the poor, feed the hungry, cloth the naked as well as other works of charity and all of that requires money.

Money does not affect one's loyalty to God, it only will help you show up what you already have. If you are disloyal, money will help you to live it out. Likewise being loyal, it takes money sometimes to display loyalty. So, it Is still very possible to be rich and yet loyal to God.

I know of many rich men who built churches, charity homes as well as donating huge sums of money for evangelization.

What makes a man disloyal to God is being too engrossed with money and not the money itself. In the bible, Zacchaeus was able to let go of all his wealth to follow Christ while the other rich men could not. Therefore, the difference is in the mind and nothing more. If you are determined to serve God, money will make it even easier for you.

A lot has been said about rich people being evil and I want to debunk that. What money does is to give you the power to carry out what you already have in mind. If a man becomes rich and then suddenly becomes evil, know that his mind has been evil but he has not been able to carry it out due to his limited power.

7. WEALTH IS FOR SOME SPECIAL PEOPLE

Just the same way a seed will germinate irrespective of who plants it, that is the same way wealth will come to anyone who follows its principles. Don't you think it will be very unfair of the universe to only reserve its abundance for some people while others are meant to wallow in peril? That's not it. Just like knowledge, money is there for anyone who seeks it. However, even though wealth is for everyone, not everyone will be wealthy. Some have already concluded that they're not among those special breeds and such self-defeating mindset will always be keeping them away from it.

This achievement of any result whatsoever begins from the mind. With the right mindset, you can achieve almost everything. So, instead of housing a mindset that hinders you from achieving financial freedom, go for more advantageous ones. Go for a more positive mindset especially in the area of wealth creation and see how it will reflect on your finances.

Chapter two

Understanding The Nature of Wealth

In the previous chapter, we talked about some of the mindset capable of hindering you from attaining financial freedom. We discussed them and also suggested a more supportive mindset that is needed for this journey to the state of abundance. Convinced that your mind is now fertile and would accept the wealth principles, let's quickly discuss wealth in its true nature.

You already know that we are on a journey, the end of which being to expose you to the power that controls wealth. For the accomplishment of such an ambiguous but simple task, the need for adequate mastery of it's real nature and forms can not be over emphasized as control comes after understanding. Except by chance, control is absolutely impossible when the system is not clearly understood.

A lot of people believe wealth to be all material and does not come in immaterial form. However, in this chapter, we will be looking at some incredible forms of wealth that many have not considered to be wealth.

Wealth is the abundance of resources of great value. It can be tangible or non tangible. The major unique nature of wealth is its ability to exert control over both resources and circumstances. With financial wealth for instance, one can do so many things. It is important for the development and better disposition of one's innate abilities. Also, apart from being able to exert the most significant effect in people's living standard, wealth is also the major basis for the measurement of success and achievement.

Wealth does not only occur in tangible form, it also comes in intangible form. The tangible forms include all material assets, cash, properties, shares, bonds etcetera. The intangible form on the other hand includes knowledge and wisdom, inspiration, influence and trust. These intangible wealths are not wealth per se, however, because they can be exchanged for tangible wealth, it will not be wrong to classify them as wealth. We will be discussing them in detail in the session that follows.

Another important point that is worth noting about wealth is that it is not self-sustaining. Wealth does not regenerate except it's acted upon by other factors. All things being equal, a million dollars will remain the same till eternity unless it is invested or acted upon by other economic factors. Likewise knowledge and other intangible forms of wealth, they instead will deplete if deliberate efforts are not being made to develop them.

WHAT DOES IT MEAN TO BE WEALTHY?

There are a series of unresolved queries pertaining to what should be the yardstick for the determination of wealth. Many economists have given wonderful definitions. Generally speaking, wealth means different things to different people, therefore, there is no generally accepted scale for its determination and measurement. What is considered as wealth to a person may not be wealth to another. A person might be worth $2,000,000 and to him, he's wealthy. Meanwhile, someone out there might be worth ten times that amount and yet he doesn't believe he is wealthy.

In the course of trying to address this intriguing area in the subject of wealth, scholars have been able to provide us with what we can hold on to in the determination of wealth. Their various definitions could be summarized as having enough supply of a resource to comfortably meet up with its demand without fear of shortage as a result of such a venture. To me, that is the most accurate answer. A man is said to have financial Wealth if he has enough to comfortably foot his bills without fear of running into bankruptcy. You have wealth of knowledge when you can comfortably give it out on demand without much brain cracking. Any resources whatsoever that you can give out at ease without fear of shortage, then you have wealth of such resources.

EXPLORING THE VARIOUS POOLS OF INTANGIBLE WEALTH

We live in a world of duality and is made up of the visible and the invisible. The visible, in contrast to how it seems stems from the invisible. As a result, it is impossible to clearly understand the visible phase without first understanding the invisible. Because the invisible stems from the invisible, it is pertinent to say that the invisible controls the visible. Coming to the subject of wealth, the intangible form also has a similar effect on the tangible. The intangible wealths are simply wealths in their raw state, therefore, there is need to clearly understand them before one can talk about the conventional wealths. The intangible forms of wealth are discussed below.

KNOWLEDGE/ WISDOM

A scholar once said that knowledge is power and to that, I would like to add that knowledge is wealth. It is the raw form of all kinds of material wealth. There is no single successful person that you can't point out to his wealth of knowledge. You can not gain financial wealth without the knowledge of finance. It is this knowledge that is then processed into the physical cash and other forms of financial wealth.

All kinds of material wealth have their roots in knowledge and no one gets to the top without it; those who do by any means definitely will go down with time. Anything gained without the right knowledge is already a failure waiting to happen.

Knowledge goes hand in hand with wisdom. Wisdom directs the acquisition and judicious use of knowledge and those who have them both will never lack anything. Considering how they have walked many people through the path of success, it will be an error in my opinion not to consider them as wealth and chase after them. They both are raw forms of wealth and should be regarded as such.

INFLUENCE

Because human beings are at the center of the wealth equation, influence seems to be the most significant form of intangible wealths. With the wealth of influence, acquisition of money and other material wealth wouldn't be a difficult task. This is because of the fact that once you can influence either of people's trust, fear, or passion, you can indirectly influence the areas in which they spend their money. Generally speaking, you must be of influence before you can make money.

Going further, sportsmen and women and entertainers are hitting it big because of their ability to feed people's passion. On the other hand, each time people fear death from diseases, doctors earn because they specialize in handling such kinds of fear. Also, if people are not afraid of any loss or damage, there will be no need for insurance companies. All these point out to the fact that influence is a raw kind of wealth and each time it is utilized, money or other forms of wealth is earned.

The acquisition of these great resources boils down to self-development. It is not just the influence that matters but the quality. What determines its value is how well it is able to meet that end to which it is targeted and because that target is usually another person, the need for the in depth understanding of human behavior can not be overemphasized. Just like in control, it is only by chance that you can influence what you don't understand. Therefore, human behavior is an indispensable course you must master to a reasonable extent if you must amass the wealth of influence.

Take time to think about this, in what areas can you influence people? Are you the type that easily dig humor out of every situation? Can you force a smile into a frown face with much ease? Maybe people can't help but clap when you sing or play those musical instruments. Do you have compassion for the sick that you subconsciously wish you could offer help? Maybe whenever you come across people fighting, you bring peace. Such influences are your raw wealth, develop and use them well!

INSPIRATION

Just like knowledge, inspiration is another form of wealth that must be harnessed before one can lay hand on any tangible wealth. More than knowledge, it is the seat of all human invention. In many cases, inspiration has helped many get to a point where knowledge can not. It is the mother of so much knowledge.

The major path to this wealth is meditation. Through meditation, our mind is exposed to infinite intelligence. It is in this realm that one can get the right inspiration to tackle some of life's challenges, including that of lack and limitations.

You can do almost everything if only you can gain the right and enough inspiration. This includes the acquisition of financial wealth.

TRUST

The common saying, "Trust no one," is simply figurative and not a complete truth. Without trust, humanity would have gone into extinction. This is because, we all need the next person to survive and without a certain level of trust, this mutualism would have been disrupted thus bringing an abrupt end to human existence.

Trust is an important commodity that you must secure if you ever dream of being successful in life. You must be trusted before you can survive in the business environment. People must first trust you before you can gain access to their valuables, this might be the reason why you have not achieved your desired level of success. Your clients need to trust you before they can award you that contract.

More than having the required knowledge and skills, having and communicating a reasonable and commendable level of moral principle is another ingredient you must have before you can command people's trust. Apart from opening you to so many opportunities, being trustworthy makes you less likely to encounter legal problems in your business. Trust is another form of wealth you need to build.

More than you chase after material wealth, take time to acquire all these intangible wealths and your financial freedom is sure.

Chapter three

PLANNING YOUR WEALTH

The importance of planning in all our life endeavors can never be overemphasized. It is the foundation upon which every achievement is built. Except by chance, nobody ever gets anything without planning for it.

Most times, Planning undergo two stages to be complete, namely:

- THE THINKING STAGE.

This stage involves sitting down to clearly evaluate all the possible required steps and the resources for the task to be embarked on. It also involves making consultations as well as critically analyzing all the gathered information. The thinking stage is mainly brain work. It is where you get the mental picture of the possible outcome of the whole task. Here are some important questions you need to answer in this stage of planning:

- Why do I need to do this?
- What is the end result?
- What are the possible obstacles?
- How do I overcome the obstacles
- What are the required resources?
- What are the processes?
- Do I have the required knowledge or should I go for training?
* Will anything go wrong if I don't do this task?

After you have clearly provided answers to all the questions, you are now ready for the next stage.

2. PROVISION STAGE

Just like the name implies, the provision stage involves providing all the mental and material requirements for the task. This stage is important, however, you don't have to get it hundred percent before executing your plan. Especially in the area of learning, there are some certain aspects of every task that are better learnt why doing the task. If you wait to be assured that everything is right before taking the first step, then, chances are that you will never move. Also, it is not a must that you have all the material resources beforehand. From your analysis in the thinking stage, you must have known the basic requirements, those that must be in place before anything can be done. Start working once all these are ready while you get the rest along the line.

Planning to attain financial freedom is not an easy one. It requires a lot and I believe you must have seen some in this book. One important fact you need to have at the back of your mind is that wealth is more a result than it is a reward. Therefore, if you want to get your desired result, then be ready to put in the required effort. There are no two ways about it! Just like I stated earlier, the universe is just in her dealings with humanity that is why in the long run, what we put in is what we will get in return. Same thing goes in the area of wealth, if you do it right, you will get it right and there is no better way to get it right than planning it right.

This chapter is aimed at equipping you with the required resources for this journey to abundant riches. Primarily, the resources for wealth creation are made up of sets of information and attitude. Every rich man you can think of has taken time to gather this information (just like you are doing now) and also exhibit a certain attitude that makes them susceptible to success. These two vital requirements will be discussed in this chapter.

13 THINGS YOU MUST DO TO BE RICH

As you are making preparation for financial abundance, it will be very helpful to consider these areas. Diligently looking into each of them will give you the stability you need to stick through until you get to your desired level.

i. DECIDE WHAT WEALTH MEANS TO WEALTH

You must have heard many people's definition of wealth and I don't want you to just pick one without making your own contribution. I need you to define it to your own taste. How much do you need before you can say you are wealthy? Let me give you some insights; maybe after you can boast of a daily capital formation of hundred thousand dollars; Maybe when you have a decent home and drive a decent car; does wealth symbolize living in luxury; does it mean being able to afford your taste of meal without having to consider the cost; does it involve having enough to live your desired lifestyle, doing your hobbies, going on vacation at will, providing all your family needs and still having something left for relatives and for charity. It is all up to you to decide your own definition.

Defining wealth in your own term gives you the sense of focus as well as giving you the required basis for self-assessment and evaluation. It is totally insane to embark on a journey without first knowing where you are going. This definition also opens your mind to the rewards attached to being wealthy and that can help to motivate you to put in all that is required. Don't forget that you can not get what you desire if you don't put in what is required.

Even as I said I will not define wealth for you, I still have not failed if I tell you to set your definition very high. If you aim high and you fail, chances are that you will still have something to be proud of unlike when your aim revolves around mediocrity. If you aim at being a multi billionaire, chances are that you will still be a billionaire when you fail which is still an honorable failure (if there is anything as such).

In addition to setting your target high, making sure that your target is realistic is still an important factor. You don't have to set an unrealistic target all in the name of aiming high.

ii. DECIDE TO BE REALLY RICH

One of the major ways in which many people tie their self dow is by deciding to adapt to their unpleasant condition. Each time you decide to settle for that, you kill the urge to press further and once you stop pressing further, you kill every chance of making things better.

Decision is the bedrock of every achievement. If you wish to achieve financial freedom, you have to decide!

Decision begins with saying to yourself, "this is what I want and I am going to work it out," followed by backing it up with action. I'm sure you must have made that decision, otherwise, will not be reading up to this point. Having determined what wealth means to you and having decided to acquire it, the next important thing is to strongly believe that you can achieve it.

iii. EVALUATE YOUR PRESENT FINANCIAL STATE

There is no way you can ever measure how far you have gone if you don't know where you started. For easy success assessment, it is important to know your current financial state. Here are some important areas you need to consider.

A. EARNING
What is your average daily earning? Because we spend on a daily basis, it is important to also measure our earning with respect to its daily value even if you earn

on a monthly basis. This is also beneficial as it is easier to calculate. With respect to earning, also measure your comfort as well as the risk level. Also:
_ Is your life endangered before you can earn any penny?
_ Do you sweat blood out before you earn?
_ How consistent is your earning?
_ Are you happy with what you do or are you just doing it for the money?
_ Is your earning adequate with respect to what you put in?

It will do you more favor if you answer these questions unbiased and with a mind free from prejudice. This will give you a clew of where you need to make adjustments.

B. SPENDING

_ How much do you spend on a daily basis?
_ How comfortable are you paying your bills?
_ Do you pay for what you really need or do you just go for what you can afford?
_ Are you living up to your desired standard?

All these are what you need to know before you can measure your success in the future.

iv. SET A FINANCIAL GOAL

A financial goal is a statement (usually written) which defines the targeted level of financial success of a person or an organization. A complete financial goal does not only explain the amount that is being aimed at, it also defines the time frame for its achievement as well as the procedure that will be followed. It is not enough to just say that you want to be rich, you should put it in figures and afterwards, decide how you intend to actualize the written figure and the time frame.

For easy actualization of your financial goal, it is advisable to break it down into smaller units. After deciding what you intend to achieve in, say, a ten years period, it is important to break it down and determine the yearly value. Breaking it further to months and to even weeks will also create more room for easy and accurate self-assessment. It helps you to know whether you are moving towards your goal or not. It also makes it easier for you to notice when and where things are going wrong and making the necessary adjustment based on the observation is also easier.

While setting your financial goal, it is very important to ensure that all the included elements are realistic. There should be no room for prejudice. You have to critically study your strength and weakness with respect to your goal and also make necessary adjustments before passing out your conclusion. Remember also to set your goal high and realistic.

v. DECIDE AND BELIEVE YOU CAN BE REALLY RICH

Everything we do in life begins with a decision. We first decide to embark on a journey even before planning for it. Believing in the achievability of a task as also another invaluable element in the success equation. So, if you must ascend to the level of financial abundance, then you must decide and also believe in yourself. The two must be present.

One of the major ways in which many people tie themselves down is by deciding to adapt to their unpleasant condition. Each time you decide to settle with what you have, you kill the urge and desire to press further and once you stop pressing further and you kill every chance of making things better.

Decision is the bedrock of every achievement. If you wish to achieve financial freedom, you have to decide!

Decision begins with saying to yourself, "this is what I want and I am going to work it out," followed by backing it up with action. I'm sure you must have made that decision, otherwise, you will not be reading up to this point. Having determined what wealth means to you and having decided to acquire it, the next important thing is to strongly believe that you can achieve it.

vi. GET A MENTOR

Wealth is such an elaborate topic and learning everything out of your own experience is not and has never been a good option. Though it is said to be the best teacher, it is not in every case. In the real sense, experience is more the costliest teacher than it is the best teacher. Imagine what Thomas Edison must have wasted before he could come up with the electric bulb, what if someone had whispered to him, "Do it this way."

EXPERIENCE IS MORE THE COSTLIEST TEACHER THAN IT IS THE BEST TEACHER

There are already laid down principles for almost every aspect of human endeavor and it is always better to follow them. A mentor will show you through those principles, why wasting time to invent a way that has been invented already?

Getting a mentor is just the same thing as getting a compass, in both cases, you are sure of a predetermined landing. Having successfully walked the same path; a mentor already knows what they have done to get there; they know the things that work and the ones that don't; as well as the pros and cons of every step. Having someone to provide you with this information will make a big plus. There is no successful person that doesn't have a mentor, even though most of them are too proud to say it. Mentors have changed the life of many people and yours will not be an exception if you choose one.

Like we learnt in chapter one, everything in this world obey the law of process. There is a process that once you follow it, you become transformed regardless of who you are and where you have been on the ladder of success. Mentors already know that process and will lead you through.

One of the major challenges that usually scare people away from getting a mentor is the fear of whether the person will agree to mentor them. Let me quickly clear the air on that. The greatest joy of successful people comes from people's admiration. Everyone likes to be admired, even the very successful people and even though they get that in quantity, the joy they get when they are admired to the point of seeking their mentorship is usually too enormous to ignore. So don't let fear hold you back. Boldly walk up to that person and make your intentions known to him and if he declines, you can still go to another person.

Another problem people have with mentors is that they are more interested in the result than the process. They love their mentors' results but have often rejected the needed discipline to stay true to the processes of the journey. No mentor will be happy to continue with unserious people, they have too tight a schedule for that. They don't have time for people who are not ready to follow instructions.

In addition to all that, it is very important that you choose a mentor from within your field. Your mentor should come from the same field with you for effective and productive mentorship.

Some mentors can be strict and that's because they want the best for you and nothing less. Therefore, instead of complaining or taking him to be too demanding, follow them no matter how it inconveniences you. You will be glad in the end that you did.

vii. DEVICE A BETTER MEANS TO INCREASE YOUR EARNING.

It is a common phenomenon that if we don't do things differently, our result will remain the same. Some people (you're not among) only complain about unpleasant circumstances and it ends there. They don't expend more energy to seek out what can be done. Many do, but stop halfway abandoning the task alongside the end result. This is one of the reasons why many people are still poor.

After you have evaluated your financial condition and you're not satisfied, the next thing is to look out for an alternative means. If you are really determined, you have to be ready to be dragged out of your comfort zone. This might involve getting more training and investing more time and money to be better at what you do. It also might involve getting an additional source of income. Quitting your current job for a better one will not be bad if you can afford that. However, in a situation where you can not, is there anything you can combine that will serve as an additional source of income? But, in a situation where your job takes all your time and still doesn't give you financial satisfaction, wouldn't it be better to consider an alternative? This, just like I would always say, is totally up to you.

Like I would always tell my students, the best kind of job is the type that pays you based on what you put in rather than your time. Productive is the best yardstick for the payment of labor. If I can achieve in one week what others are achieving in one month, it will be unfair if I don't get what they are getting in one month. I refuse to settle for any job where my earning is fixed no matter what I put in.

IF I CAN ACHIEVE IN ONE WEEK WHAT OTHERS ARE ACHIEVING IN ONE MONTH, IT WILL BE ABSOLUTELY UNFAIR IF I DON'T GET WHAT THEY ARE GETTING IN ONE MONTH.

Working under fixed earnings is having another man decide how much you will ever make in a lifetime and no one has ever become wealthy under such a situation. No one has ever become wealthy out of another man's decision.

However, standing on the corridor of manhood, it is not bad to start out under this condition, what is bad in my own judgment is not planning to be your own boss. Of course, everybody must not be a boss but everybody can decide to get paid based on their output and not time input. Wrapping it up, to increase your earning, you will need to:

_ Improve at what you do. This is mainly effective if you're self employed.

_ Get an additional source of income. In this case, prioritize getting a passive income stream.

_ Opt for result-based payment.

You can adopt as many as possible.

viii. DISCIPLINE YOURSELF

This is where most people miss it. There is a common saying that without hardwork, nothing grows but grasses and I want to add that there can be no hard work without discipline. It doesn't matter what you have, if you don't maintain the necessary discipline for the effective and continuous execution, you still will not get your desired result. You can get all the motivation in the world but, without discipline, you are going nowhere. This explains why someone can be more successful than the other even though they have the same mentor and have equal opportunity. Motivation will bid you 'go', while discipline will help you to keep going. Both are important in the journey of life.

If you must be truly wealthy, here are some attitudes you must discipline yourself to overcome.

- Laziness

I hate bearing bad news, but many people are just too lazy to be wealthy. Laziness can be mentally or physically, or even both. Being wealthy requires being mentally and physically alert. Get any rich man to tell you the work he is putting in or have put in before becoming wealthy and you will be shocked. The world is just too blinded by the result, that is why it will only tell you that Elon Musk is the richest. It will hardly tell you about his sleepless nights, his years of wandering and the so many beasts he had confronted.

It is out of laziness that many are trapped in the pit of easy life mentality. Stating it bluntly, if you don't face the hard life, there will be no easy life for you. Easy life is not easy, it is only meant for those who overcome the hard life! Behind every fascinating glory is a scary story. Study anyone that genuinely earned his riches and you will understand better. Behind those luxurious meals are days of junks; behind those expensive holidays in a distant land are years of working round the clock, behind those enviable achievements are loads of deprivations. That is what it is!

Now that you have decided what wealth means to you, are you willing to put in whatever that will be required to acquire it as long as it's ethical? Are you willing to stick to your plan until you see the end result? Are you ready to wake up early and go to bed late just for that additional result? If you have answered yes to all the questions, then read on.

Here are some practical ways to overcome laziness in case you're still battling with it:

_ Set your task right.
_ Time yourself. You should be able to set the time for the completion of your task and most importantly, be realistic.
_ Get all the necessary requirements. Both the material and mental tools.
_ Get someone to account to. This could be a family member, a friend or an associate. You can also use your social media status. Telling people what you want to do and when you intend completing it can help stimulate the zeal to meet up. I have tried it out myself and it did work.

EASY LIFE IS NOT EASY, IT IS ONLY MEANT FOR HARD PEOPLE

- Procrastination.

This is another monster you must overcome. It has deprived many people of their life-changing opportunity. It is a leading cause of such an outcry like, "I wish I did it earlier." The blame is not the problem, the problem is still continuing the old way.
One question you should always ask yourself each time you are tempted to say later is WHY NOT NOW. Why can't I start now?

- Inconsistency.

Imagine you came back from work after a very stressful day. Famished, you rush to the kitchen to prepare something. Lucky enough, you still have some stew left in the freezer so you only need to cook rice. Then you brought the quantity you needed, set it on the burner, turned on the gas and started cooking. After some seconds, you bring down the pot to boil water. Then, after the rice pot has gotten cold, you place it on the fire again and start cooking. Then you keep repeating the process. Cooking rice requires a steady heat supply for some minutes and you are violating those principles, so, it will be wiser to to forget about dinner that night. I believe you must have gotten the gist.

If you really want to succeed, then be ready to make consistent effort. Making consistent effort does not only involve steady input, it also involves making sure that all the input complement each other and are playing a given role to the achievement of the desired end. Like in the above story, putting the pot of rice over the fire and bringing it down are both input, but an antagonistic one.

• Indecisiveness

Every life's achievement is a product of decision, so you must decide if you must achieve. It does not end in making a decision, your decision should be followed consistently.

• Pessimism

The human mind is so powerful and can work wonders. Everything it mind holds for some time definitely happens, be it to your favor or against you. If you think about success, then you will be successful, if it is failure you think, you will fail. You can't climb the ladder of success with a mind full of failure. Therefore, instead of thinking how miserable it will be if you fail, fill your mind with how amazing succeeding will be.

One bad thing about pessimism is that it will pick only the worst possible outcome and then magnify it to a point where it drains your willpower. Once this happens, chances are that you will quit the whole process and even if you don't, you begin playing not to lose instead of playing to win. This is one of the major differences between the rich and the poor. While the rich are confident in his ability and believe that they have all it takes to win, the poor are often gripped with fear and are more focused on the things that are likely to cause them failure. If you enter any business with such a mindset, the best you can ever get is just your capital and nothing more. Discipline yourself to be optimistic, it pays.

YOU CAN'T CLIMB THE LADDER OF SUCCESS WITH A MIND FULL OF FAILURE.

---

ix. MINGLE WITH LIKE MINDS

As you begin thinking of creating more wealth, it will be important to look for people with the same goal. This is because the people you mingle with have a very significant influence in every aspect of your life. To this, keeping mediocres as friends while thinking of abundance is a very wrong combination.

If you think of becoming a millionaire, the best people you should mingle with are millionaires, but when you don't have anyone close to you, you should at least go for people thinking about the same. One of the major reasons for this is that what you hear always matters a lot. The kind of conversation that often goes on around you will tend to exert a very significant influence. It doesn't matter whether you agree with what they're saying or not, the words you hear don't just go like that, they're there either in your conscious or subconscious mind and tend to form a belief system with time. That's why you need to only mingle with people who are optimistic about life.

Keeping friends with people who are on the same journey with you has so many benefits. With like minds, you can easily share ideas and make positive contributions to each other's success; you can share your challenges and be sure of getting support, either morally or otherwise; with them, you get more constructive than destructive criticism; and lots more. Such friends have a lot of benefits, they can give you the push you need to press further even when you're at the verge of backing out on your plan.

x. YOU NEED TO BE RICH MORE THAN YOU NEED TO LOOK RICH

If people should devote their energy to being rich just like they do to looking rich, the world will be full of millionaires. Many people, especially the youths are more interested in looking rich and oftentimes not putting the required energy to be rich. Dressing richly is not bad on its own, what is bad is doing that just to show off and at the cost of your financial success. It is common to see people who break into their savings just to buy the latest clothes. They often do that to measure up with a certain class of people, people who in most cases are only buying those latest fashions with their excesses. One thing is common with people who spend time meeting up, they often end up eating their seed trying to meet up with people who are only eating their fruit.

I have studied rich people's lifestyles and I discovered that the latest clothes, the latest cars and the classy lifestyle don't move most of them, except for celebrities. I also learnt that those of them who chase after all that are only doing that with their excesses. Even celebrities live their classy lifestyle for business purposes, of course some of them make millions from tickets to every show.

As you set out for the journey to riches, you have to forget about looking like you are rich. Dressing like the rich doesn't make you rich, it will only make you poorer. Just wear a decent dress with a decent smile, you make all the impressions you need.

xi. STAY UP TO DATE

The world is evolving on a constant basis and to continue being relevant in your field, you must move along with the trend. To move with the trend involves going for new ideas and staying up-to-date with the recent development. Attend conferences, seminars, listen to relevant podcasts, you never will measure exactly how beneficial those little pieces of information will be to you.

xii. CONTROL YOUR SPENDING

Being able to spend only based on need is an invaluable attitude. Reckless spending is one of the greatest enemies of financial growth. And someone might ask, "what else is money meant for other than to be spent?" Money is not just meant for spending, it is meant for judicious spending. If you keep spending each time you have the impulse to do so, then you are cutting your chance of accumulating wealth.

It is common to hear that "buy it" bell ring in our head and I am going to tell you what to do. When next you hear that, ask, "Why?" and see if you will get any reasonable answer. You will discover that the answer most of the time will boil down to gratifying an already formed habit and not based on necessity.

Some have already automated their spending. Their TV subscription is on auto renewal; their data subscription is on auto renewal, etcetera. Those companies introduced those mechanisms to continuously suck you and to make paying them your top priority. The worst part of it is that whether or not you exhaust your current bundle, you will still be renewed at your own expenses.

If you are really interested in changing your financial status for the better, then here are the things you need to do.

_ Cancel those auto renewal plans. It helps you to reconsider whether you want to renew them and when.

_ Set your scale of preference and spend starting from the uttermost necessity.

_ Spending should not come first. First decide how much you will save before you begin to spend. To this, I would recommend that you form it as a habit to always keep aside ten percent of your earnings before you begin to spend. That is some of the greatest finance advice I have ever received and I'm glad to share it with whoever is interested in learning it. You might never know how important those little amounts you are keeping aside will be until you see an investment opportunity in the future. That is when you will realize how good it is to have something to start with and not having to borrow all the required penny.

Savings will be discussed later in more detail.

Another source of wastage could be from electricity, always TURN OFF any appliances that are not in use. You can as well go for those that are built to save more energy.

xiii. MAKE OUT TIME FOR SELF-ASSESSMENT

After you have put all these measures in place, it is important to determine when you will have to assess your success. This will help you to know whether or not you're making progress.

Chapter Four

STEPS TO WEALTH CREATION

When I started dreaming of pulling myself out of the shackle of poverty, the first thing I did was studying different successful people. Having understood that if I could replicate what they did, chances are that I would get an exact result. With so much enthusiasm for a better life, I began studying them as a matter of necessity. I watched many interviews, read biographies, as well as books written by many renowned CEOs. In my series of studies, I found out that there are three things common to all of them and that I will be sharing with you in this chapter.

As ambiguous as wealth creation might be, those men were able to hit it big by employing these steps_ the same steps that have been in existence for ages, lifting people from the same position you've been dreaming to be lifted from.

The difference between you and that wealthy man out there is just the knowledge you acquire and how you put that knowledge into use. If you believe this to be true, do you think you will be rich if you follow the same steps as the rich? Your thoughts are as good as mine. But, don't forget I said, "FOLLOW the same steps" and not, "KNOW the same steps." This is because of the fact that success is action-based and does not depend only on acquiring and acquiring more knowledge. In fact, as beautiful as knowledge is, until it translates into action (s), it will NEVER bear any tangible fruit. It does not matter how many years you spent learning how to swim, if you do not move your limbs on getting into the stream, you will still drown alongside others who never attended any swimming class. The same thing is applicable to success. If I had studied all those noble men without executing what I have learnt from them, there still would not be any difference and maybe, you wouldn't be reading this book now.

Having thrown your mind into the state of readiness to grab and execute these golden principles, I present to you the three steps to wealth creation:

STEP ONE: DISCOVER A PROBLEM

Problem discovery comes in form of asking certain questions such as:

- What do people need?
- Is there any product people struggle so much before they get it?
- Is their any product or service that requires an improvement?
- Is there something I can do to make life easier?
- Are people facing a distance barrier accessing any market?
- In what ways have I been helpful to people around me and can I monetize such help?

These and many more are the questions to ask in the problem discovery stage of wealth creation. To get them more better, you may need to engage in a discussion with friends as well as conducting a research.

STEP TWO: DESIGN A SOLUTION

Designing a solution begins with answering the questions raised in the previous stage. Note that you can only do better focusing on one question or few related questions. This is where most people get it wrong, they want to do this and that and they end up doing none. Although diversification is good in the process of making wealth, but it can not take the place of competency. You are not going to be paid based on how many things you do, you are only paid for what you can do better, what you are competent at and people are ready to pay for.

Designing a solution can be very problematic, this is where the boys are separated from the men. Every body can discover a problem but it is not everybody that can design a solution. Many will begin the process but only few will stick through until they get their desired result. It takes a whole lot of time and resources to get a viable solution, however, the reward you stand to get in the end is worth it. That is why I would always advise you to never quit searching for solution as long as the problem remains.

STEP THREE: SELL YOUR SOLUTION

Because the motive remains wealth creation, the designed solution must have market value. It must be something that can be exchanged for money.

Wealth creation, be it from real estate, marketing, health, product creation and all other commercial activities is primarily based on these steps. First, you have to discover a need that is calling for attention; a situation that demands modification and then devise a means to put it in order. Need is the major thing that brings about spending for those who feel the need and earning for those meeting the needs. In real estate, for instance, the basis for wealth creation is meeting the people's need to secure properties. If such a need never existed, there wouldn't be anything like the real estate business. Need and by extension, problem, is the bedrock of wealth creation on that account, problem solvers are the highest and the most genuine money makers. Necessity, they say, is the mother of invention and invention is the mother of wealth creation. To create wealth, you must either invent a product or a service and that happens after a problem has been discovered.

Reading further, you will discover some salient truths that will change your perspective about the problem. Each time you encounter a problem or see people encountering a problem, there are opportunities to make more money, provided there is something that can be done about such a situation. Seeing how true this is and how often I have gained from it, I began loving problems for each time I resolve them, they always make me a bit richer_ either material or immaterial, or both. If only our eyes can be opened to the opportunities, fortunes and rewards embedded in the problems and challenges of life, we will all begin to embrace them more than we avoid them.

For every problem solved, you gain what you ordinarily wouldn't have gained should the problem be taken away.

We all have our individual problem, but there are times when the easiest/only way to get ours solved will be to lay it aside and help others solve theirs. I am not speaking as a philanthropist or a humanitarian, I am talking business. Let's assume your problem is lack of money and you have a rich neighbor who has been visited by other pains of life and is depressed, then your problem is half solved once you discover that. Instead of wasting in your pain, the wisest thing to do will be to keep your money problem aside and look for a way to knock some relief into your rich neighbor's heart. I bet you that once you are able to achieve that, you will be surprised at how he will help you solve your own problem. Even though this does not always happen instantly, you have made a contact that will definitely count someday. Aside from that, there is this feeling that comes with being the reason behind someone's smile. Such a feeling reduces anxiety and can give you the strength you need to press further.

We don't only make money by solving a private problem, we also earn from a generalized problem. That is even when we earn most as the value of a solution is proportional to the number of people it is serving. If the problem is only faced by a few people, then it may not even be a business opportunity. Conversely, if a whole nation or nations face a problem, such a problem becomes a gold mine.

During the 2020 covid-19 lockdown, a friend of mine told me how he earned his one year revenue within a space of barely three months. What did he do? As markets were locked up and people's movement restricted, he opened a home delivery service and started helping people get their basic goods right at their door steps. Being a very strategic marketer, he opened a website where people can easily place orders and from that, he was able to attract more traffic than he has ever done. That was how a PROBLEM transformed his business into a mighty empire_ At least, 90% of the new customers he attracted during the lockdown still patronize him till date due to the quality delivery services he made available to them. In addition, it was out of the problem that he discovered a better way of doing business and generating more traffic. The covid-19 was to him a gold mine.

Another friend of mine also became a millionaire from producing hand sanitizers and face masks. We met in Florida a couple of months earlier and he told me he lost his job. It was a terrible moment for him and he thought he had gotten to the end of the road. To make matters worse, then came covid-19 with the restricted movement and everything. However, immediately the Word Health Organization recommended alcohol based sanitizer, he decided to utilize an opportunity, having read chemistry. He broke into his savings and also got some loan from friends and began producing hand sanitizers. The business brought him so much returns that he was able to clear up the loans in three weeks, to his greatest amazement! Today, he's living fine with his family, the covid-19 just turned his life around.

The covid-19 pandemic remains one of the worst catastrophes ever in the history of human existence. Lives were lost in several millions and business activities grounded, but that was when the two young men met their breakthrough.

Every mind blowing invention was born out of mind draining necessity. All the genuine world millionaires were born out of pressing needs. I will give you an account of some of them.

Alexander Graham Bell discovered the problem people face to pass their message across. From there, he labored until he was able to come up with a device that put an end to the problem. His invention was what gave birth to smartphones and some other hand devices we use today. Of course, you can't ask me what happened to his financial life afterwards for you already the answer.

Mark Zuckerberg saw the need to create a more user-friendly platform that enables people to communicate and share thoughts and resources from across the world. After a series of trials, he came up with facebook and today, the whole world has been unified. In just a millisecond, one can send and receive messages from any part of the world. For the problem he has solved, Mark has risen to be one of the world's richest men.

Wealth creation is not a rocket science, it is all about being responsive and strategic. Being able to sense needs in the environment and making strategic moves to address them. My first business was selling animal feeds. I was not even up to eighteen then.

Discovering that there was no feed store around and we can only get it from the nearby city, I decided to cease an opportunity. First, I needed to test how fast the business would be moving so I met Mr Jack Donaldson, our immediate neighbor and told him I can get him feed whenever he is in need of it and he will not have to drive miles just to get it. He was so happy with the offer and told me he will be needing some next week. I also met Mr Jones and he also accepted the offer. I met so many people and the result was encouraging.

Although not all the people I met responded positively, I was sure the business was going to turn out good. Then, I began advertising my new business with the help of my social media handle and I was amazed at the sense of relief from my would-be customers. Being a decent young boy from a well respected family, getting them to trust me wasn't a task. My wealth of trust just helped out and they began placing orders without any doubt. I added the money I realized from their upfront payment to what I already had and I was set for business. By taking care of the people's burden of getting feed for their pets, I began making some cash everyday. So much that I no longer ask my parents for money, except for bigger needs I can't attend to.

The truth is that there is always something you can do. It must not be something entirely new or different, you can modify an already existing idea. You can start up a business with well improved customer services. You must have heard how some people display dissatisfaction with certain brands, so creating a similar brand and addressing those areas of dissatisfaction will give you an edge. This does not only apply to product dealers, you can be so good at your job that everyone wants it done by you. I can still remember how my father would pass so many mechanic workshops just to meet one Mr Christopher. Mr Christopher was one of the few mechanics that after servicing your car, you can be sure it has been serviced and you are not going to face the same issue any time soon. As a result, my father wouldn't mind taking public transport for weeks just to have him do what "only Mr Christopher can do better," according to him as he is usually occupied.

When you are good at what you do, people are ready to inconvenience themselves just to have you attend to them. This means that it does not end in getting the problem solved but doing that to people's taste. One of the things people fear most in business is competition, especially when there are so many people doing the same business. However, here are some tips that can make you stand out:

6 SECRETS OF MASSIVE SALES

i. GET YOUR FEASIBILITY STUDY RIGHT

You don't just go into a business without first all studying the viability of the business. In your feasibility study, some of the most important areas to be looked into include the target market (the people you intend selling to), the market size (their population), the already existing brands that will be your source of competition, etcetera. This information will tell you whether the intended business will be profitable or not.

ii. PLAN YOUR BRAND PROPERLY

Nothing prevents poor performance like proper planning. After you have gotten a green light from your feasibility study, the next thing will be to plan your brand. Brand planning has to do with bringing components that will make you stand out in the crowd, something there will make your brand draw traffic to itself. Getting this done, you can be sure of a very good return.

iii. SET YOUR PRICE RIGHT

Price is one of the major determinants of every business transaction. It is the major tool for business traffic control. Setting your price at a point where your clients don't feel cheated is very important. To keep your price moderate, try cutting out unnecessary production expenses. Once this is achieved, recovering your principal cost will not be difficult even with your added profit. Your profit should also be kept at moderate, it is better to even minimize profit and maximize traffic than scaring customers away with outrageous prices. In addition to traffic maximization, there are situations where selling below your target profit level will speed up the growth of your business. For instance, let's say you buy a piece of furniture at the sum of $200 and you intend selling it at $600, but on getting to your shop, someone offers to pay $400, then it will be wise to take the $400 and go and buy two more at $200. By doing so, you have achieved a sales advantage over that fellow who is determined to hit his target. Also, you have doubled your goods within a very short time.

iv. PRIORITIZE CUSTOMERS' SATISFACTION

Customers are the engine that drives every commercial activity. Because these engines are human, you must take out time to understand them. This understanding is what gives you the template you need to satisfy them.

To keep your customers coming and even helping you promote your brand by referring it to others, you must put in all that is required to satisfy them more than other brand owners, provided it does not violate the business ethics. Everybody wants to spend his money where he will get the best out of it, so you must always have this at the back of your mind.

Having a good sense of humor will be a bonus for you. People love to transact in a very friendly environment. In addition, also learn to wear a smiling face when dealing with your customers, it is very important. But in whichever case, do that when it is required.

v. EYE-CATCHING PACKAGING

Just like product description, packaging is another important area you must get right if your brand must sell. People are attracted to what they see and your packaging should be catchy enough to do that.

Generally, here are some factors to consider before designing your packaging material and style:

- For whose consumption is your product?
- Is it meant for adults or children?

Children are more attracted to classy and shiny objects than adults. They're also moved by colors therefore, products meant for their consumption should have as colorful packaging as possible. Unlike children, adults are not so much moved by colors. However, the packaging material has to look nice.

Consider also whether your product is gender based. If yes, is it for men or women? If your product is for both genders, which gender is the major consumer?

Putting all these into consideration will help you adopt a Packaging that will be appealing to your major target customer.

vi. MAKE YOUR BEST BETTER

It is one thing to be the best and another thing to remain the best. Although it is not possible to remain the best forever, however, you can prolong it.

I have taken time to study why many people get to the top only to find themselves at the bottom the next day. From my findings, I discovered that the major reason is relying on one's best without further attention to improvement. If you must remain at the top, there is every need for constant improvement. Make your good better, your better, best and your best, more better. With that, you can be sure of prolonged lead at business and everything you do.

The motive of problem discovery and solution development is for wealth creation. However, solution development does not result in wealth creation, wealth comes after you are able to sell your solution. Because of the serious competition in the business environment, the above strategies should be put in place to create the edge you need to scale through in selling whatever solution you have developed. By 'solution', I'm referring to all kinds of products and services.

For business owners, creating more wealth is dependent on them. They can decide to apply strategies that will increase sales; those under real estate, or even cleaning services for instance, can decide to speed up and to reach out to more clients so they can increase their earning. However, if you are working under a boss, speeding up and doing your work more diligently alone can not increase your salary unless your boss decides so. By deciding to increase your workload by yourself and to do it more efficiently, you are only making extra dollars for your boss. If you are thinking that doing all those things will make him notice you and make a move for your pay increase, it doesn't easily work that way. Your boss is less likely to decide on a pay increase unless you initiate the conversation with him. This is where it gets scary for most people. They fear that they might be insulted or even fired should they demand for a pay increase. The truth is that such things should not fear you. All you need is to follow the right approach. You need to first put yourself in a position where they are afraid of losing you to another company.

Honestly, no boss is comfortable with the idea of giving out raises. Such additional cost is what they would like to avoid as much as possible. However, when you make the work environment smoother for them and also contribute very significantly to the progress of the firm, you can be sure of getting the raise if you demand it. The key note is that you have to be up and doing first before getting a pay increase will be possible.

PART B

WEALTH PERPETUATION

"It takes a matchstick to make a fire, but it takes a million trees to keep a fire."

~ George Donald

Chapter five

ADOPTING A HEALTHY FINANCE MANAGEMENT

Proper finance management is an act that must be mastered by anyone who admires wealth. It is the key ingredient to creation and perpetuation of wealth. Even though money is inanimate, I love to liken it to a farmer's birds that requires constant care and attention. Once the right care and attention is given, the farmer can be sure of sustaining a generation upon generation of flocks. On the contrary, if it gets to a point where the farmer begins to deny his flocks the needed attention, he will lose it all no matter the number.

Like we said in chapter one, money is a result of an action and to keep it flowing, you must not interfere with the action. This is just a rule and it must be followed. Remember when you first dreamt of making money, you probably first remembered that money does not grow on trees so you started looking for the right place where it can be found. You began to search until you found your first dollar. You then repeated the process and you got another one, then, you were like, "Wow, so this is it, I'm gonna keep it on."

We all have a similar experience. At one point or the other, we seemed to be so eager and passionate about making and making more money. Some were able to follow the right procedure and they did find the money. However, not everyone was able to sustain it. Looking around the neighborhood or places you have been, you are likely to notice people who were once doing well financially but today, are simply surviving. Majority of such cases can be traced to poor finance management. Some were as a result of one mistake or the other while for some, it was due to failed health conditions but whichever way, we will be discussing some finance management practices that will cut down your chance of running into the same problem.

To have the full knowledge of finance management, these are the key areas that must be clearly understood:

Earning
Spending
Saving
Investment of savings

EARNING

Earning is the first area to be put under control and the first thing to achieve in this regard is steady earning. Because spending is steady by default, a system or combination of systems that allows for steady flow of income should be put in place to meet up and to even super pass. This can be achieved in so many ways but because we are looking at being wealthy, I only advocate for the right kind of employment that can guarantee that. Some kinds of jobs can give you steady income but can never give you financial freedom not to talk about being really wealthy. For instance, we know doctors, lawyers, and company workers to be earning on a steady basis and some of them are enjoying a decent and comfortable living with that but, that is not what this book is advocating for. Living comfortably and financial liberty are two different things. You can be living comfortably, yet without financial freedom. Gaining financial freedom means living above financial limitations and it is far beyond a mere comfort.

Like we said earlier, you have to prioritize jobs that offer you a system of leverage and also pays based on your level of productivity and not based on the time input. That was the same system that has raised all the world's multi millionaires you know.

In addition to that, having a multiple stream of income is also very important. Some really rich people have gotten to a point where they allocate their various individual expenses according to their different sources of income. They have gotten to a point where a particular income stream is for family upkeep and another source, for another set of needs, and another, for investment. They also have created systems that earn money for them even while they are asleep. Most importantly, the super rich millionaires have successfully created a system that keeps them from worrying about earning. Earning, to them, is what happens by default such that they can spend the rest of their lives on vacation and their financial freedom will not be hurt.

SPENDING

As long as a man lives, the demand for spending is by default. There is a constant demand from all kinds of bills, demands you can not neglect easily. In this phase of finance management, the goal is not to terminate it (spending) because it is not possible, the goal is to put it under control. You must first learn the act of controlled spending before you can ever get to a point where spending is no longer a threat to your finances.

Controlled spending is the first secret to financial freedom. Unfortunately, this is where most people get it all messed up. They simply earn, spend and then remain broke until they earn again. Most of them simply go broke because when they had some, they couldn't clearly distinguish between needs and wants. The only way you can control your spending is by drawing a boundary between needs and wants and after that, building the required level of discipline to maintain the boundary. Many people spend under pressure, they spend not necessarily because they need to but because of the spending habit they have formed.

If you are just starting to build wealth, you need to learn to only spend on the needs among your needs while you postpone the rest. This is where the highest level of discipline comes in to be able to meet up with the required denials and delays. But, remember I said 'postpone' and not 'cancel' because each time you do so, that little voice will continue to suggest to you why you don't have to wait but meet such needs. You need to constantly remind that little voice that you will meet the needs when it is most favorable.

As you are just starting the journey of wealth creation, postponing spending does not mean that you don't have the needed finance but because there are more productive areas that demand so.

YOU MUST FIRST LEARN THE ACT OF CONTROLLED SPENDING BEFORE YOU CAN EVER GET TO A POINT WHERE SPENDING IS NO LONGER A THREAT TO YOUR FINANCES. CONTROLLED SPENDING IS THE FIRST SECRET TO FINANCIAL FREEDOM.

In spending, always make sure that the satisfaction you will get in return is worth the price you are paying. It wouldn't be much wiser to pay so high for a product when you know you can get the same brand and the same quality elsewhere at a cheaper rate. You don't need an exotic boutique because you wouldn't be wearing their tag around. It is true they usually deal in quality stocks but it is also true that there are other decent shops dealing on the same quality.

I am not by this teaching that sticking to average is what will make you rich, I am only advocating for the judicious use of your hard earned money. Anyways, it is your money and you have every right to use whichever end you wish but I still need to talk to you about getting the best out of it.

In spending, always spend on quality and durability, it is always cheaper to do so. Yes, you heard me right. Quality stocks are cheaper than those of less quality. A quality cloth will outlive two or more poor quality clothes and in addition to that, it will also speak more positively about you. Remember, you will be addressed the way you dress. Likewise other materials, it is always better to go for quality because each time you go against that, you are going against your comfort and sometimes your self esteem.

Extending it to feeding, sacrificing your taste wouldn't make you richer. Even if it is not for taste sake, for the sake of your health, you always need a healthy meal. Don't joke with that. You know your health is the primary thing. Health goes before wealth and you need to be alive and healthy before you can enjoy your wealth. What you don't need is a constant dinner at the most expensive hotel, you only need that once in a while.

SAVING

There is no better way to prepare for the future than to leave a portion of whatever you earn. Apart from the sense of guarantee it gives, constant savings provides you with what you need for future investment. It also gives you or at least some fraction of what you need to cease a business opportunity that ordinarily would have passed you by if you were to start from the scratch looking for every needed penny.

If you must ever get to a financially free state then you must learn the act of saving. If you are expecting to just stumble on a billion dollars someday, remember that Elon Musk and other genuinely wealthy men in society did not make wealth that way. They started from saving and then multiplying what they have saved. Besides, even if a big bag loaded with dollars should fall from your ceiling, you will still lose it because it takes discipline to sustain wealth and saving a portion of whatever you earn is just one of the many other forms of discipline you need to be able to sustain wealth.

Some people often mistake saving to be something for the really rich and financially free individuals, but that is not it. The truth is that you even need it more than those financially free individuals who have already created systems that constantly replenish whatever they take out of their pockets. So, no matter how little you are earning, still try to keep something aside. If you wish to grow financially and you are hoping to get a little push from someone, then you have to start ahead of time to first give yourself the little you can.

Just imagine stumbling on a business opportunity that requires a hundred thousand dollars but you have to beg for everything. It will be so unserious of you.

However, it will be more reasonable if you have even if it is just a little portion of the needed capital. It will even make you more bold to ask for help.

If you really desire riches, then you have to start saving and there is no better time to start than now. You might be saying, 'oh, it is too late for me to save, I would have started earlier.' Now that you have seen the importance, don't listen to that little voice. Start saving, no matter how little. Start saving, no matter your age and no matter the inconveniences, you will be glad you did when you will look back and see how much you have been able to accumulate.

Okay, let me assume you are comfortable with what you are getting that you don't need any future investment, but take time to consider these:

- You will definitely grow old someday and you won't be able to work anymore. When that happens, would you like to survive at the mercy of others? Will anyone be willing to pay for that luxurious life you've always enjoyed?

- What if there is an emergency tomorrow, how will you cope? Maybe you develop a health challenge that requires surgery urgently, will you be able to raise the required funds instantly?

What will absorb the shock it will cause to your finances?

- What if you run into a legal case?

- What if there is a recession?

The list is unending, each pointing out a reason why you should begin to save. Saving, to a very large extent, insures for the future, and if this is going to be your only reason, then you don't need to read the next subheading which is investment of savings.

THERE IS NO BETTER WAY TO PREPARE FOR THE FUTURE THAN TO LEAVE A PORTION OF WHATEVER YOU EARN

Below are some of the most effective tips that will help you to master savings.

i. PLAN FOR IT. You need to first determine how much of anything you earn that you will save. It will be good if you put it in percentage. You are in the best position to determine the figure that will be most convenient for you.

ii. CREATE A REMINDER. Just like other habits, saving is not easy when you are first starting it. You are likely to forget it sometimes but creating a reminder will be of help.

iii. SAVE BEFORE YOU SPEND. Always remove the portion you have decided to save before you begin to spend. If you first go into spending, chances are that something might pop up that will require you to remove from what you intend saving. To make it easier, you can make saving automatic.

INVESTMENT OF SAVINGS

My father forced the habit of saving into our head at a very tender age. I can still hear him telling us to always keep a portion of our pocket money, that it will make us grow as rich as he was or even more if we should continue to do so. Then, my only motive of saving was to be as rich as my dad which means I will be far richer than all my mates. That was exactly most children's motive of saving.

Saving, in real life, does not make someone rich. Ah! But a wise saying has it that a penny saved is a penny earned? A penny earned is not the same thing as a riches earned. If you really want to earn riches, then you must have to force every penny earned to earn another penny and the earned penny to earn another penny. That is where investment of savings comes in. There is no better and faster way to make wealth than investment. Please, I am not talking about investing in a get-rich-quick scheme. What I mean is that you will get wealthy much faster if you can get every penny you are not using at the moment to join you in the wealth making process.

Instead of seeing your savings as wealth, see it as your army of laborers. Each of the pennies is your laborer and a laborer is not meant to stay idle. Of what use is your laborer that is not working for you? I think this should be the apex of finance management, getting all your idle money to start earning you more money.

YOU WILL GET WEALTHY MUCH FASTER IF YOU CAN GET EVERY PENNY YOU ARE NOT USING AT THE MOMENT TO JOIN YOU IN THE WEALTH MAKING PROCESS.

Apart from savings, there are times when you will need to source for money by other means for a high return investment. Saving alone will not always be enough for every investment and then you might need to sell off some of your properties. In addition to raising the needed capital, an intense study should be conducted before making any investment so you don't lose your hard earned money. You are to take time to study all the risk factors and most importantly, be sure you have the necessary knowledge of what you intend investing in. If it is a new business, take time to do your feasibility study. We have already talked about feasibility and the areas you should focus on in the previous chapter.

On the other hand, if it is a company that you wish to invest in, you also need to study the company critically. In such a case, you need as many details as possible. You need to know beforehand the company's strength and weakness; their possibility of growth; their net worth; their future challenges such as whether there is a very powerful competition coming up; their tax history; etcetera. Most of this information can be found in the company's balance sheet. You need all the details so you don't invest where you wouldn't be able to get back your money plus the profit.

This study can be ambiguous therefore, it will be wise to make consultations. Ask to be clarified in any area you don't understand and never act on assumption or half knowledge. There is no better place to get the right advice than from your money mentors. So, it is very important to discuss your new investment plan with them and always follow their instructions strictly. I will take it again, always follow their instructions strictly. Remember, your mentors have been there before you and as a result, they can see far beyond what you can see. They know when an offer is truly what it claims to be or it is just meant to lure people to their financial doom. Your mentors are able to critically analyze facts and figures more than you can. It might be your emotions dragging you but they are too mature for emotional attachment when it comes to business. Therefore, it will be a very big risk to neglect their advice.

Chapter six

KEEP IT STEADY

Like we previously discussed, everything you see is a result of what is happening in the background. Wealth, fame, and anything you can think of. Since a light is a result of a flame, it is important to keep the flame burning for as long as you still enjoy the light.

There is usually an urge to relax at a certain level of progress but the fact is that relaxing usually results in decline. After you have gotten to the top, it is good you stick to the process that took you there. Those efforts should still be maintained. Such discipline as punctuality, total dedication should continue and for anyone you can't continue with due to one reason or the other, don't fail to get someone to fill that space. If your work demands starting by 9am and can't meet up to that anymore, make sure there is someone to 'fill your space.' Also, as you will likely be absent from work due to one reason or the other, make sure that your manager and other necessary staff are duly informed of what to do.

The world is constantly evolving. New ideas are coming on a daily basis. Almost everything is improving for the better. This brings about the need to move with the trend. There is every need for constant reassessment and improvement if you must maintain your space in the commercial world. Look at the automobile industries, there was a time when Volkswagen was the trend. Today, is it still the case? Even in telecommunications, there is a drastic shift from what we had previously. There is a constant modification and new products are taking over. All these point out to why you must keep improving on your source of riches. There is every need for every necessary adjustment so as to continue meeting the needs of your market. Failure to do so will amount to progressive decline and to extinction because competitors who are able to move with the trend will take your place.

The more money you have, the harder it is to handle or rather, to protect. Especially at the first time. As you are making your desired financial progress and intending to keep it up, there will be temptation here and there. That is when you will begin to see many alluring opportunities, most of them promising instant doubling of whatever principal you put in. You will begin to notice more ads offering one get-rich-quick scheme or the other. An african proverb has it that he who has a palm frond is whom goats will follow. The more money you have, the more noticeable you become to fraudsters. Those guys can be smart and can disguise anything. You must not fall for them and the best secret to escape their sugar-coated lies is by not giving them your attention. What gets your attention will with time begin to make sense to you. That is why they will keep coming and coming for as long as they are getting it.

In addition, don't allow greed to creep in. It makes one more vulnerable to fraudsters. About 95 percent of their victims failed because of their greed and negligence to the law of process. You are smarter, I know. I know you are going to stick to the process. You have not forgotten that you got to the top by hard work and only with harder work will you climb higher.

A singer whom I respect so much once emphasized in one of his songs on the need to be good to the people on your way up the ladder because you will need them on your way down (Lucky Dube, The Way It Is). There are people who have played one significant role or the other when you were starting out and some of them are still there. Some of them have sacrificed a lot to see you through and you sincerely need to continue holding them in esteem. Some of them might not have attained your level of success but they still remain an irreplaceable figure in your success story. In this case, you need them to remain at the top. Okay, you can still do very fine without some of them but certain relationships are irreplaceable. Not necessarily because of what you still stand to gain by sustaining such a relationship but because the joy of every success is carrying each and every one of the contributors along.

Your parents are one of such people you must not take for granted for whatsoever reason. They saw you through from the very beginning, when you were totally helpless and defenseless and could not do anything for yourself. They were there for you. They walked you through childhood and sacrificed a lot to see you through maturity_ their comfort, their resources and sometimes, their happiness. Yet they did not give up. You can not imagine how happy they are for your success. They are proud of you even if they are in the land of the dead. If your parents are still alive at the point of your success, you don't know what God has done for you. It is your time to pay them back for all they have done for you. Can you really pay? You should reward them, rather, and will there be enough reward? You just have to show them that you really appreciate them.

Your siblings are yet another set of people you shouldn't forget. Remember those sweet memories you both shared. In addition, there are people whose influence contributed so much in making you what you are. People like your mentors and advisors. Your success should not cost them your loyalty because you will still be needing them from time to time.

The strength of every organization lies in their level of relationship. To keep a relationship flowing, each member has to be given a sense of belonging. It doesn't matter what position he occupies, as long as he is making contributions, he deserves to be treated with some respect. The CEO owes all his associates down to the company's cleaner some respect. That is the kind of spirit you need to instill if you want all your subordinates to work as a team. It will make your workplace a more conducive environment thereby enhancing productivity.

By now, you must have gotten a financial planner because it is one of the most crucial actions you can take to manage your wealth more efficiently. A good financial planner will assist you in making sound investment, retirement, and insurance decisions. They will also be ready to address any queries you have concerning account management. Their role in your finance management can not be overemphasized.

Getting a competent financial planner can be so demanding, however, here are some of the key tips to securing one at much ease:

Ask anyone you intend to employ for their credentials and take time to study it. It is from there that you can determine their level of experience. What you need is not just an ordinary worker but someone with the required qualifications and expertise to do the work successfully – preferably, someone who has been in business for a long time and has consistently won excellent marks from clients.

It is also important to ask for references from former employers or clients and make sure that they each have had a personal relationship with your candidate.

Another effective way you can grow perpetual wealth is by helping others to grow. The more you invest in people, the more you build help in advance for yourself should anything go bad in the future. I am a living witness to this. My late uncle was a very successful business man and was one of the richest in my town. While he was alive, he was a well-known philanthropist and has invested in many people, especially poor youths. Many, he saw through school through his scholarship scheme. He also had raised more millionaires than anyone in town and had begged numerous humanitarian awards. Later on, there was a fire accident that destroyed almost all the shops in the market and his three shops were involved. To make matters worse, this happened two days after he just stocked the whole shops with goods for Christmas. He was so traumatized, having lost almost everything.

The bad news spread like wildfire and people were very sad that such a thing had happened to such a nice person. His boys (the people he had built) began trooping in their numbers with different kinds of gifts, reassuring him that everything will be alright. About a week later, they came again, this time in a group, about fifteen of them. After thanking him for all he had done for them, they presented him with a cheque of twenty million dollars. They had secretly raised the money from a freewill donation among themselves.

Raising people is indeed raising oneself above failure. What you invested in others will definitely stand for you someday and in most cases, this happens when you might have run out of hope, when the situation is tough and you just need help badly.

It is also important that you remember your initial motive for wealth, which I'm sure wasn't to prove a point or anything other than the satisfaction it brings. Therefore, there is no point flaunting it. The truth is that the world is just too busy and flaunting your wealth just to get their attention is likely to be a total waste of resources. You don't need to impress anyone, you just have to be yourself and stay true to yourself. It is totally wasteful to buy expensive things that you don't necessarily need just to show off. Use that money to create more wealth instead or invest it in charity homes when it will be highly needed.

If you continue working hard and focusing on your investments, you are sure to create perpetual wealth.

Chapter seven

SECURE YOUR WEALTH

I will need to say it again, secure your wealth. This is where the stereotype about money increasing someone's level of insecurity emanates from. The more money you have, the more you become a target to fraudsters and scammers. However, the truth remains that you can get over all that. After all, I have never heard of Elon Musk being scammed.

Securing your wealth is a task only you can do better because you know better what you passed through to get there. So you alone can give the required care. This is where perpetuation of wealth lies. This can be demanding, but it is something you can do. After all, it is not more demanding than wealth creation, which you have achieved.

There are a number of ways to secure your wealth but we will be looking at the most effective ones.

MAKE LONG-TERM INVESTMENTS

One of the best ways to secure your money when not in use is by investing it. This does not only offer you the needed security, it also allows you money to increase in value. You can invest in properties of different kinds, stocks, shares etcetera. In whichever way, remember to first get the approval of your financial advisers before making any more. Refer to the previous chapter for more details.

QUESTION EVERYTHING

In order not to run the risk of losing your hard earned money, you need to be extra careful. Always ask questions and don't act unless you get a satisfactory answer. People like to judge this as being paranoid but who really cares. It is your money you are trying to secure.

LEND MONEY WITH CARE

Do not lend money to anyone unless you are sure of getting it back. Always know the cause for which the person intends borrowing and don't give out your money unless you are convinced by the chances of returns. While giving out loans, you have to have the best interest of the borrower at heart and not just the interest you stand to gain. People are more likely to pay up loans once they succeed in the business for which they obtain the loan. On the contrary, if the person did not succeed, you will have issues getting back your money. Even though the loan is secured against a property, you may not like to sell it, maybe because of your relationship with the person. That is why it will even be better not to give out loans to your relatives unless you are ready to accept the worst should it happen.

BUILD MORE ASSETS

Creating more assets is another effective way you can secure your wealth. It increases the stability of your wealth and also creates room for wealth expansion.

Other effective security measures includes:

- Having as many income streams as possible.
- Being cautious while making online payments.
- Signing your check yourself.

You have to prioritize securing your wealth so you don't lose it.

THE RIGHT PLACE TO START

Throughout this book, I have been leaving you to decide things for yourself. However, for the first time, I am going to plead that you permit me to decide for you or rather, tell you what to decide. I need you to decide to start somewhere, that is the best place to start. Though I will be pleased with you testifying that you have learnt a lot from this book, I will be much more pleased if you will say, "I'm going to implement what I have learnt."

Starting anything new has never been an easy task and it takes courage to determine to start whichever way, and the truth is that until you start it, you will always remain at point zero. One of the major problems we normally face when starting something new is not knowing where to start. Just like you took out time to think until you decide on what to do, you can as well decide to start somewhere. Starting somewhere might entail starting with something quite different from the initial goal.

After I had decided to go into piggery, which has been my dream business since my high school days, I was much hindered by lack of capital. Pig production is a capital intensive project indeed. Right from setting up the building, getting the breeding stocks, buying the feeds and providing the needed medications. To be sincere, I was almost drained when I did the cost analysis.

To make matters worse, I had no one to assist me and I did not intend to secure a loan. However, I remembered that I could start anywhere. With the money I had saved from my feed business, I was able to set up a snail farm. It was paying well and afterwards, I added a poultry farm. The both farms generated nice returns and after the first year, I was able to erect a small house for the pig production. Because I had not saved enough money, I couldn't stock it that year.

My initial target was just three breeding stocks, so the building wasn't that much. The next year, I stocked the farm and began fully and today, I smile each time I look at my poor beginning and the level of progress I have achieved. That gigantic Bluewhale Farm just started as a small enclosure behind our family house. It started as a small snail farm.

If I had waited or saw my financial insufficiency as an excuse, I'm sure I wouldn't have gotten to where I am today. I may not even have started.

This is not a cooked up story. It is a true life story, my own story at that! It is intended to inspire you to look for where to start. You can start somewhere and you alone can find your most convenient starting point.

Just start today and in a hereby future, you will be so glad you took that decision. It is my most sincere pleasure to see this book inspire you.

I wish you the best of luck.

Yours George Donald

www.ingramcontent.com/pod-product-compliance
Lightning Source LLC
Chambersburg PA
CBHW070244220526
45465CB00004B/1518